LLOYD BECKMANN, *Beekeeper*

TIM STITZ AND
KELLY SOMES

CURRENCY PRESS
SYDNEY

CURRENCY PLAYS

First published in 2011
by Currency Press Pty Ltd,
PO Box 2287, Strawberry Hills, NSW, 2012, Australia
enquiries@currency.com.au
www.currency.com.au
in association with
La Mama Theatre, Melbourne.

NATIONAL LIBRARY OF AUSTRALIA CIP DATA

Author: Stitz, Tim.
Title: Lloyd Beckmann, beekeeper / Tim Stitz and Kelly Somes.
ISBN: 9780868199146 (pbk.)
Subject: Drama.
Other Authors / Contributors: Somes, Kelly.
Dewey Number: A822.4

Typeset by Dean Nottle for Currency Press.
Printed by Hyde Park Press, Richmond, SA.
Back cover shows Tim Stitz.
Cover photographs by Talya Chalef.
Cover design by Emma Vine, Currency Press.

Contents

Lloyd Beckmann, Beekeeper was first produced at La Mama Theatre, Carlton, on 3 February 2010 with the following participants:

LLOYD / GRANDSON	Tim Stitz

Director, Kelly Somes
Lighting Design, Bronwyn Pringle
Composition and Sound Design, Liz Stringer
Sound Design and Realisation, Neddwellyn Jones
Aroma Design, Jodie Ahrens
Design Concept and Realisation, Tim Stitz, Kelly Somes and Ashlee Hughes
Production and Stage Management, Jessica Smithett

Dedicated, with thanks and gratitude, to Lloyd Stitz for allowing us to tell his story.

The creative team would like to especially thank Jane Woollard (Dramaturg/Director's Mentor), Max Gillies (Performance Mentor) and Michael Howard (Landscape Consultant) for their contribution to the work. The development of this project was made possible with the support of HotHouse Theatre's *A Month in the Country* initiative.

Subsequent performance seasons: Free-Rain Theatre (Canberra Theatre Centre, February 2010), La Mama Courthouse (April/May 2011), Tamarama Rock Surfers (Old Fitzroy Theatre, Sydney, June 2011) and Brisbane Powerhouse (July 2011).

PRODUCTION NOTES

Smell

Aroma design is used in this work. Aromas such as honey, eucalyptus and hinoki (an aroma which resembles the disinfectant smell of hospitals and aged-care facilities) are emitted from a 'smell machine' into the performance space. Moments in the play where aromas are emitted into the space are indicated in the text.

Characterisation

The character of Lloyd talks directly with the audience. There is an element of improvisation in his engagement with the audience. These moments are indicated in stage directions rather than written dialogue.

Structure

The performance has no interval or formal scene changes but the script has been broken into sections and given titles to denote thematic shifts.

CHARACTERS

LLOYD, an elderly beekeeper
GRANDSON, late 20s–early 30s

Both characters are played by the same actor. Changes between Lloyd and the Grandson are signified through idiosyncrasy, physicality, voice, costume, light and sound effects.

SETTING

The play is staged in an interactive theatre environment. The space is dressed to resemble a granny flat—Lloyd's home. The audience is seated in the granny flat on armchairs and couches surrounded by Lloyd's possessions, including his knick-knacks and family photos. The audience are immersed in the performance space—they are invited by Lloyd to sit on his favourite armchair, touch his family photos, eat his honey, drink his beer and smell the honey wafting from the extracting shed outside.

NOTES

Please note that the shifts in tense and punctuation, particularly commas, in Lloyd's dialogue are intentional. These are present to indicate idiosyncrasies and the rhythm of his speech.

In line with this, a number of words have been spelt, used incorrectly or abbreviated.

THE WELCOME

The audience are gathered outdoors, outside of the performance venue. Bee boxes are strewn around 'the yard'.

SMELL: Smoke from bee smoker.

The sound of cheery whistling and the song 'Be Happy' playing on a portable cassette player becomes audible. LLOYD *emerges from a smoky spot outside, dressed in his beekeeper's suit, hat and gloves and carrying a bee smoker. He puffs some smoke towards the audience in jest and compares this act to smoking bees in the hive to pacify them. We can smell* LLOYD*'s aftershave—Imperial Leather.*

LLOYD: Oh, you're here! I'm overwhelmed. There's so many of you.

Lloyd Beckmann Stitz. And you are?

He continues to introduce himself individually to audience members. He gives the smoker, hat and cassette player to audience members to hold as he arranges himself.

So you're here to learn about the bees. Beekeeping, well it's a science, it's also considered an *art*. Over the years I sort of… I've always tried to progress and later I studied the breeding of queen bees, which is the grafting of the egg.

Okay, back to basics. This is how it all starts.

He points at the hives.

The reigning queen bee would have laid a host of eggs and these are here in all the cells.

He indicates with an old honeycomb frame.

He hands the frame to an audience member to hold up.

And she'd go along and lay one, two, three, to one thousand a day. Each egg is resting on a bed of royal jelly. What's royal jelly?

Bee's milk. Doesn't matter if it's a worker bee, a queen bee or a drone bee. They all start out the same. And each egg hatches into a larvae, a grub.

You with me?

Having asked the question, he doesn't allow anyone in the audience to respond.

Now, the old queen is three years old. She's a bit long in the tooth and the bees want a new queen, a young beauty. So the nurses begin to construct queen cells or queen cups.

These are bigger than standard cells and are at ninety degrees, perpendicular to the frame. Like this, but these are synthetic queen cups for queen breeding. I won't go into that.

So the nurse bees put an egg in the queen cell and feed it profusely with royal jelly.

Now when the cup is chock-a-block with royal jelly, the grub would roll over and it would cocoon itself, like a chrysalis, and turn into a bee. But because of the profuse amount of royal jelly they'd produce a queen.

In nature, the first queen out, she'd eat her way out of the cup and rip all the other queen cups down. She'd rip 'em down and kill 'em; because she is number one.

The old queen is still in the hive, the bees either kill her or kick her out the front door: 'Go on, Mum'.

Any questions? Good.

Well then of course, her new royal highness's got another duty to perform. After another three, four, five days or whatever, she'd go out the front door. The nurses would've preened and tidied her up and she'd go up into a congregational area, outside the hive, roughly about ten o'clock in the morning.

He looks at his watch.

It'd be done by now.

And the drones, the males, from all of the hives in the local area, they go out to defeciate…

You know, have a shit!

He winks specifically at one audience member, a young bloke.

And of course this young queen is coming out, the first one that can grab her and mate her and then inseminate her, that's it!

He slaps his hands together.

They mate in the air, and after she's satisfied, he dies. Because she latches onto his penis and he can't get away from her. When she's got her fill, she pulls away taking his penis and he falls from grace. He carks it!

She goes back to the hive and the nurse bees tidy her up and get this penis out. But she's probably not satisfied. She'll go out again the next day or maybe twice that day if she's a hussy, until her spermatheca is full of sperm.

Then the cycle begins again and she's ready to begin the good work of laying. You up to speed?

So, her eggs come down the spermatheca and they only get a wipe of sperm for fertilisation, and this makes them a worker. All worker bees are female and the queen is the high priestess. She'll then continue to lay thousands of eggs per day until she runs out of sperm, in her autumn years, she might be two to three years old. When she runs out of sperm her eggs are not fertile and those eggs become drones, the males. That's how drones occur.

But the problem is then this hive would begin to decline. They'd have stacks of drones—slack bloke bees who just fly and fertilise—but not enough workers. So the remaining workers would start to breed up new queens and the cycle begins again. The first new queen out, she rips the unborn queens apart and the old mum gets kicked out the front door: 'Off you go to die in the field'. You clear? Good!

[*Realising he's got carried away*] Sorry. I've gone off on a tangent.

You asked why I'm so interested in bees. How did I know I wanted to be a beekeeper? When I was three or four I went to my uncle, Henry Beckmann's place. Out the front he had rows and rows of white boxes; forty hives. That's two million bees. Fifty thousand bees per hive. In a strong hive you could have sixty to a hundred thousand bees. That's a lot of bees! I thought it was fascinating. You could hear the happy buzz of the bees. Buzzing here and buzzing there. They were happy! Well I was sucked in! It planted bees in my mind. Bees have a mystique: the sting, the barb, the nectar, the pollen. But they're social beings you know. One bee wouldn't survive on their own. They need the hive, the colony, and the beekeeper. That's me!

COME INSIDE THE HIVE

LLOYD: Okay, enough questions Tim. You need refreshment if you are going to continue the hard, hot work of beekeeping. Take up your hoofers. Come on; get up off your ass. Welcome to Château Lloyd. Miner Kleiner Haus. This here is my hive.

He invites the audience into his home (the performance venue). He leaves some of the bee paraphernalia on a table inside the door. He asks the audience to sit down and make themselves at home. He turns off the reel-to-reel tape player, which has been loudly blasting sound around the granny flat.

Introduce yourself to the chappy or *fräulein* next to you. This here is our new colony.

He moves in amongst the audience, speaking to them.

Now let's get you all a drink.

He picks out a young female audience member to assist him.

You, young *fräulein*, can you give me a hand?

You can have a fruity white, cask wine I'm afraid, a Four-X for you blokes or butch lassies, or tea or coffee or water. And there's some little nibbles there next to you.

He points to bowls and jars of biscuits and lollies situated on the furniture around the granny flat.

Help yourselves. Go on. All you gotta do is ask. It's all here for you. If you don't ask then it's not my fault if you want for anything.

And there's only full cream milk, don't have any of that fake stuff. Only full cream! That's what I grew up on. None of this half fat, reduced fat, skim, soy milk. I was born and bred on yoghurt and cheese and… ninety years, all pure full cream milk! And here I am today at this age. Has that cream or that yoghurt done any harm to me?

He oversees things being organised in the kitchen.

You okay in there?

He notices his young assistant from the audience serving drinks.

All you young people, you're very fast, always on the go. Rushing here and rushing there. I was driving down the road to Kenmore Village, and these young people, hoons, they were tailgating me and then they went shhhht, in front of me, barping their horn. It made me red hot! I was absolutely incensed. You young people gotta be considerate of us oldies on the roads. I can still drive though. Went for the test, passed with flying colours. The eyes are good. Got my hearing aid. I can still drive Tim.

He shows the audience where things are in his home, his music.

Dialogue ad-lib.

He shows the audience where his Bee Journals are and his Reader's Digest collection and volumes of books. He mentions an article where planes full of bees are flown to the US to pollinate their crops.

He points to some photographs.

These here are some of my grandchildren, the brood. Here's Clark's kids. Tim, Simon and Annabelle. More where that came from, there's Russell and he has Kate, Claire and William, named after my old man. Wilhelm. [*He spells it out.*] That's W.I.L.H.E.L.M. Wilhelm. It's the German variant for the name William. And Diann and Tom, the Browns, they have Stacey and Todd and a new one called Angus *Lloyd*, fresh off the press, and you know who he's named after.

He points to himself.

A chip of the old block.

He sniggers.

Jean, my wife, calls them our little celebrities. Jean's not here right now. She's getting to be a bit of an old bee like me. She's had a few falls so she's up the hill in Haven Lodge in high maintenance care. Being looked after by the nurses. Good workers, hard workers. I'm down here in this box, solitary confinement. No.

He laughs.

I go up to see her on my whiz-ding scooter, you probably saw it outside, oh no, you probably didn't, it's in the garage today. I need a flag though. People don't see me coming. It's a four-wheel scooter!

Anyway, I am packing up some of her things.

He points to Jean's things in boxes.

Downsizing. Happens to all of us. We all lose our sting, knees, hips, back, marbles…

He refers to photographs on a table next to his armchair.

This here is Jean, my wife, and my grandson, Tim.

GRANDSON: That's me.

LLOYD: That's my son, Clark. He was Royal Australian Navy Fleet Air Arm. Pilot Lieutenant Commander, flying Skyhawks and Trackers off the aircraft carrier *Melbourne* before decommisionment. He's not here anymore. Blowing with the wind now.

The GRANDSON *picks up the photograph of Clark.*

Pause.

GRANDSON: You look so much like your dad.

LLOYD: You look just like him, Tim…

Pause.

He places the photograph back on the table next to his armchair.

He picks up his beer and raises his glass to the audience.

Cheers! To your very good health.

He and the audience drink.

He settles into his armchair.

So, Tim, you asked how I knew I was to become a beekeeper? Well you could say it was my destiny. My early days of beekeeping I recall, I was approximately seven years of age… and we were living in Ipswich. And we had a lemon tree out the front of the house and I was very interested in why these bees were all in the flowers of the lemon tree you see, gathering nectar. And I tried to, I got a wooden safety matchbox and somehow or other I caught a bee. I put it in the matchbox and well, I thought I had a beehive.

Now, I couldn't work out why the bee wouldn't stay in the box and why it wouldn't make honey for me, I was only seven you see. I would try and catch another and put it in there too but as soon as I opened the box the other one flew out the other side. So… it didn't happen because the bee obviously died and there was no queen in there and it was a matchbox, a ruddy matchbox. But as the years rolled on I was always very interested in bees…

There are many ways of extracting honey but you got to have the gear to do it. This here gear, it's time to pack it away. Too old. I act as a consultant to beekeeping colleagues and the like, but it…

He stops mid sentence. He senses there is someone at the door. He goes over to open the door. No-one is there.

Hello?

DE-ROBING

Transition moment. The actor transforms from LLOYD *into the* GRANDSON.

SOUND: Fade up 'De-robing' by Liz Stringer.

LIGHTING: The mood has changed dramatically. The granny flat has changed from warm and inviting to cool and blue.

The wind blows into the space. It is the breeze from up north. The GRANDSON *breathes in the air. It is filled with memories, with the past, questions. He undoes the beekeeping suit.*

As he steps into the room spotlights come up on individual pictures of Clark, Lloyd's son. He is everywhere. The GRANDSON *walks through the granny flat looking at the photographs. He arrives at the photograph of Clark next to Lloyd's chair. He picks up the matchbox, strikes a match and lights a candle sitting aside the photograph.*

The GRANDSON *takes off his grandfather's shoes, his feet are bare underneath. He places them on the ground in front of him.*

He peels off the white beekeeping suit and stands in his underwear and singlet.

He billows out the beekeeping suit onto the ground in front of him. He watches as the air slowly drains out.

He picks up the beekeeping suit and folds it up. He sees Lloyd's hat and smoker, collects them and places them in pile with the suit next to Lloyd's armchair.

He picks up an old electric shaver next to Lloyd's armchair.

SOUND: Fade up 'Passing Down' by Liz Stringer.

GRANDSON: [*impersonating Lloyd's voice*] Your father gave me this.

He turns the shaver on and puts it to his cheek and shaves in jest.

[*In his own voice*] Dry shave, wet shave.

He opens the cupboard next to Lloyd's chair and pulls out a container of Johnson's baby powder. He puffs the powder into the air, puts some in his hand, and pats it under his arms and in his crotch.

[*Again playing with Lloyd's voice*] Got to stop the chafe.

He laughs.

He picks up a bottle of Imperial Leather aftershave and slaps it onto his neck and cheeks.

[*In his own voice*] Sex scent… For the ladies…

The GRANDSON *sees one of Lloyd's shirts and a pair of beige pants hanging behind Lloyd's armchair. He removes the shirt from the coat hanger, looking at it with curiosity. He puts it on. He also tries on Lloyd's pants. He sits into the strangeness and unfamiliarity of wearing such high-waisted pants.*

[*Impersonating Lloyd; trying on his persona and mannerisms*] You see!

He sees a pair of Lloyd's good shoes and puts them on.

He sits down in Lloyd's armchair. For a moment he places his young hands next to the old shoes. He feels the worn leather of the shoes.

[*Impersonating Lloyd's voice; exploring the different registers and rhythms*] When I walked into the mines I had to get new shoes… had to convince my stepfather I needed them. My own father, Wilhelm, W.I.L.H.E.L.M., died when I was three years old. At the age of thirty years he contracted typhoid fever and succumbed to the disease on the fourteenth day of August, nineteen hundred and twenty-two. He had become a very good road and track racing cyclist and was held in high regard by all known to him, as far as I can tell. I didn't know him.

He does up the top button of the shirt. He moves over to the mirror to consider his reflection. He removes the mirror from the wall and moves into the centre of the granny flat.

LLOYD: Hello there… Sexy devil.

[*Recognising a familiar reflection*] Hello there… hello Clark.

GRANDSON: [*interrupting, searching*] Dad? Dad, why?

He touches his ears. He explores his receding hairline. He notices his hands in the reflection and puts the mirror down.

[*Impersonating Lloyd's voice*] We have the same hands but Clark and Tim, theirs are soft. Not of the land. Mine are worked and lived long. You can still see the stings in these hands.

He looks at the palm of his hand and begins to trace the lines (the life line).

Transition moment. The actor suddenly transforms from the GRANDSON *into* LLOYD.

LLOYD: [*aggressively*] You were soft if you wore gloves. A sissy.

SMELL: Gum/eucalyptus.

Cheers. If you haven't sucked it all back by now. Alcos!

THE HARD PAST

LLOYD: So as the years rolled by, bees were always a constant. I remember my brother Merv and his mate used to ride on horseback through the forest. They'd take a scarf out of the tree, with the axe on the side of the saddle; they'd take a scarf out of the tree and mark it. And you're riding a horse you see, the horse would walk along and you, it wouldn't matter, you didn't fall over because you were watching up, looking up at the sky and you could see the cloud and you could see the bees in the trees. It was bees in the trees, and there was a hive in the trees, and they'd be all going in and out you see gathering nectar. Well next Saturday or next weekend, we said, we'll come back and we'll fall that tree and we'll get the honey.

So they'd light a fire with cow manure around it so that it would smoke, so when the tree fell, the smoke would smoke the bees you see. Pacify them.

You'd fell the tree and cut it open and here'd be all the honey in this trough. So you gathered that and you put that in a sugar bag, a clean sugar bag, which was hessian sack, and then you'd hang it up in the shed. And, of course the hot sun, the heat of the day, would make the honey run through the sack and into the pot, so here'd be your honey. That's how you gathered honey in those days.

You follow the trees, the blooms. Fifty to sixty percent of beekeeping is knowing your flora. Pollination. You can make an absolute coin from that bizo!

SMELL: Gum/eucalyptus fades out.

I can see you're getting thoroughly bored with me. You've got to sample the product. The fruits of my loins. Nectar of the Gods. Here you go, pass it around. Liquid gold. Wacko! No preservatives, keeps all on its own.

He gives out honeycomb and honey on Jean's collector set of souvenir teaspoons.

He shows the audience the honeycomb.

This is the honeycomb.

GRANDSON: Can you eat it?

LLOYD: Yeah! You can chew this stuff, like the bees, till it's soft. Make your own hexagonal cells and cluster them together and make your own honeycomb, or you could just put it under your seat.

It takes about five hundred bees four weeks to collect enough nectar to make just one kilo of honey. Beekeeping is a slow and steady process. The bees, they work and work and work.

Well then I got to the stage where I wanted a hive of my own. This was at sixteen years old. At the time, my mother had died, my stepfather kicked me out, put me to work. It was the Depression you see, no money, so I became a ward of the state. I got rations that way. I really wanted to work in the mines, like my brother Merv, but you had to be eighteen years to go underground. So I went around farms and asked 'Got any work today?'

Every Saturday though, on my free time, I used to ride my pushbike about three miles out to this chappy's place. I knew him from primary school, he taught me. They had a calf club and a poultry club, you can imagine, and well I was part of the bee club. He was quite happy for me to help with his bees.

All around the verandah of his old Queenslander, a house on stilts, he had hives of bees facing out through the railings. Plus, he had this front bedroom with the old Victorian double doors leading directly out onto the verandah and this was his room for honey extracting. In his house for Pete's sake! And of course I thought this was great, and I'd spend all of Saturday with him and his bees. His bees got to know me; my smell, my pheromones.

So from him, I finally got a queen bee and some bees and a little nucleus box, like the one out the front—but it was an old kerosene box—and that's how I started my first hive… I became a beekeeper! Those were the days…

I got to the stage where we were married, Jean and I. We grew potatoes and other vegetables. Well we always had our own honey. I used to have the hives out in the bush because our neighbours at the time didn't want to have bees next door. [*Imitating his neighbour*] 'Oh, they'll sting our children…' Stuff that! How girly can you get?

Well this particular time, it broke her heart a little bit, Jean's heart, broke my heart a little from that point of view. I would send this honey, my honey, down to Brisbane to the Roma Street market and I got the docket back to say that I got threepence a pound for the honey but because of the charges for the freight and all the rest of it, it didn't leave me with much dividends for all my effort… and this annoyed me naturally, and during those years, the price of honey was very poor. Not too many people really produced a lot of honey, because nobody wanted it, you couldn't sell it.

And so, I, I sort of had a bit of a break for a period, a long period of time. I just kept my couple of hives here and there.

Pause.

He puts the honey and honeycomb away and refills his glass of beer.

I was sixty-four when I got back into bees properly. Things weren't right at that particular time of my life, financially. I went from a big house in Ipswich to a ruddy caravan.

I'd cashed in my super and with a mining colleague we bought a mining rig for prospecting coal deposits. Black gold. Exploration! [*Beat.*] Look, I made a series of bad decisions. It's a long story… [*beat*] my colleague screwed me. He sued me. He wanted out, so I had to buy out his share of the mining rig. And compensate him for the trouble. But I had no equity to pay engineers and staff to run the rig. So I sold it. And lost money.

On top of that we, Jean and I, had bought land in Paddington, in the city, to build four townhouses on. Our nest egg. We built the townhouses, but no-one would buy them. We eventually sold them too, but we lost more money on them. Jean, I don't know if she ever forgave me. She used to have a new handbag every week, wads of cash in her purse. She was… bitter.

I had to go back to what I knew. I got back into primary production. It's like Jean's dad said, old… ah, what's his name… oh hell… I lost it. Oh dear, this's terrible. He's my father-in-law. Um…

He's straining to remember.

Ah, Jordy, the Scotsman, he said, [*in a Scottish accent*] 'Yoo cannae liv on lurv yer know'.

I had no money. We lost a lot of money. The bank took the beach house in Coolum, the car, even some of the furniture Jean and I got after we first married. All we had left fitted into that pokey caravan.

I was devastated. But my grandson asks, 'Why? How? What happened exactly Grandad?' I should have had my retirement! I was just down; I was just about killed as far as that goes… Nothing left in the tank.

I was wrecked, mad, crazy. I was dangerous and mixed-up. I went down to the hospital and sat in the waiting room, [*looking around the audience as if they are the people in the waiting room*] but I thought I don't need to be here. I went up to the mining club, to show my face, get support.

He slams down his beer.

I had been a first-class colliery manager, qualified by the Department of Mines and the State Electricity Service! But I was sixty-four—who's gonna take me on? I had to go back to what I knew. Pawpaws and honey and vegetables. I did it to make money. [*Zoning in on an audience member*] Only reason I did it mate was because we were broke, absolutely flat…

He is a little unstable on his feet.

Well they used to come up, they, the old, Standard Charted Finance used to come up, once a week, they'd send this character up [*imitating the accountant*] 'Have you got any money for us today?' Just like a cane toad waiting for the bees to leave the hive.

He gulps, imitating a cane toad eating bees.

We just didn't have any money to give 'em. Because this stupid mining character let me down. He'd bent me over a barrel. I was in chains.

[*Aggressively zoning in on another audience member*] Who's going to go out there and work in the hot sun for nothing?! Only because of the love of beekeeping!

My kids helped as they could, Russell gave us a pot to piss in and some land to put the flaming caravan on and eventually he built a granny flat for us. Diann helped. She set Jean's hair every week with rollers. Clark helped, he left the navy and moved up here to help, but in the end he had to protect and provide for his own family and went to Melbourne.

DISEASE SPREADS

SOUND: Fade up 'Disease Spreads' by Liz Stringer.

LLOYD: Then the disease spread. My hive collapsed. Clark fell over too at that time. He and Gill, his wife, were involved in a big car accident. A smash in Sydney. A drugged-up, drunk truck driver careered into them. Lost his baby daughter. Only three months old and they almost died too. Their car was mangled, bulldozed, nothing left. The boys were with their grannies in Canberra thank God. And Clark and Gill were up in Sydney showing off the new baby. It just fell apart. [*Pause.*] No-one knew how to fix it.

Clark took himself away to die.

He flew off across the fields and towards the sea.

He stands up straight and does a military salute. In a slow physical transition, his saluting arm draws down and the GRANDSON *slowly presses his fingers up under his chin, resembling a gun.*

Snap—suddenly LLOYD *wrestles back control from the* GRANDSON.

You know, such is life. You gotta keep smiling.

He puts on a large Luna Park smile.

You got to stop that thing up there.

He points to his head.

Messes you up. It's like a disease. A Foul Brood. It sits in the bee's belly and eats them from the inside. The light is sucked out of the hive. A dark empty box. Tiny carcasses in black disfigured cells.

SOUND: Fade up 'Disease Spreads Further' by Liz Stringer.

It kills both your larvae and your pupae, like my grand-daughter and my son. You got to push it down. Push it down into the ground.

He becomes overwhelmed. The grief takes over and becomes too much.

Transition moment. The actor transitions from LLOYD *into the* GRANDSON.

The GRANDSON *moves around behind Lloyd's armchair and lifts up the seat cushion to reveal a mess of stuffing contained within. He digs into the armchair and pulls out the stuffing with his hands. He holds up the grimy and coffee-stained stuffing and studies these straggly innards of the armchair, as if they represent a painful personal and family history. Suddenly he cannot hold them any longer and stuffs them back into the armchair as he speaks, and finally replaces the cushion.*

GRANDSON: You gotta burn the hives and the bees and bury them. Clear the lot. The disease finds a way to keep going. You got to push it down into the earth, cover it over, so it don't come up again.

Pause.

SOUND: All sound suddenly stops and all is silent.

Mum came to meet us under the rose arbour. 'Daddy's dead.'

Red rose petals fall from the ceiling.

Pause.

We wrapped our arms around each other, clutching so as not to let go, but somehow it was never far enough. Our arms were too short. We were missing the wide arm span of you Dad.

SMELL: Mango and pawpaw.

Push it down?

He fears this repression of emotion.

LLOYD: [*knowingly*] You gotta push it down…

GRANDSON: [*angrily*] Push it down?

Transition moment. LLOYD *wrestles back control from the* GRANDSON.

LLOYD: You gotta push it down…

LLOYD *sits gently into the chair.*

LIGHTING: Return to the warm, domestic comfort of the granny flat. The isolated and cool shades are gone.

PAWPAWS

LLOYD: It was a killer, an absolute killer…

You know it's a silly game. It's like all primary production—it's like me with the pawpaws the same way, you know, twenty years out there growing pawpaws and I couldn't sell the blessed things. It's all about how the product looks. Mine were tainted. Mottled and blemished. It's like honey, the paler the colour of the honey, the more money the buyers will give you. No-one's going to buy an ugly pawpaw or dark honey. I could sell my pawpaws to the nursing homes because they were peeled, easy on the dentures. The accountant said, 'You're mad! The pawpaws are losing you money. It's time to finish.' You say to yourself, how silly. I look back on myself and how bloody mad I was… So I had to dispense with them. Burn the lot. Four and half thousand pawpaw trees. The whole plantation.

I still do them. I still love them… You've got to move on.

[*Announcing to the audience*] Who wants some bloody pawpaw? It's homegrown. I still have a small crop. My grandson thinks they smell like vomit. Delicious.

Also got some mango for you wimps that don't like pawpaw.

He gives out mango and pawpaw to the audience.

R2E2

LLOYD: [*holding up a mango for the audience to see*] This mango is what they call the R2E2.

They've mixed a smaller variety of mango called the Kensington. [*He spells it out.*] K.E.N.S.I.N.G.T.O.N., Kensington, with a larger breed, the Brazilian, to build a bigger, sweeter mango.

The mangos got opened up to the world market, like the honey. So it's not all bad news. Aussie producers, we're the best in the world, pure. Fair dinkum. As comrade Rudd would say, fair squeeze of the sauce bottle. What would the gingy lass from Wales say? We gotta 'move forward'…

I used to supply Capilano, who were and still are the co-operative beekeeping people… I'd send them forty-four gallon drums of honey, at a price whatever they gave me. Gradually I built up to a hundred and fifty hives.

This was in my retirement, after the big losses. The money I was getting from the honey was going back into the business all the time. I had to buy timber, buy frames, buy this, buy that. We were surviving on the dole. Jean on the seniors pension and me on the invalid pension. I'd wrecked my back and knees in the mines, you know.

SMELL: Mango and pawpaw fades.

I started going around to shops and that wasn't a very successful situation. I tried selling my wares on the side of the road for a bit of cash, sat there in my big hat.

He sees a young fräulein *in the audience who takes his fancy. He moves over to her.*

Then I started going around to Chinese restaurants, and the Chinese folk of course, they wanted honey because of their ability to, all their, honey pork, honey chicken, honey prawns, honey this, honey that; [*lasciviously to the young* fräulein] they use a lot of honey.

He goes to his desk and gets out examples of Chinese takeaway menus and sidles up to another young fräulein *from the audience.*

I had my mates down at Kenmore Village, Asperly, Billy Liu and Sammy Chung and Gilbert Lau down at Indooroopilly, you know [*spelling it out*] I.N.D.O.O.R.O.O.P.I.L.L.Y., Indooroopilly. That's Aboriginal for the local area.

I got started with them and I went from one Chinese restaurant to the other until such time…

He moves his hand onto her knee in a very 'familiar way'.

But I had to be careful that I didn't overstep the mark in as much as that if I couldn't supply them and let them down, they'd have to get it elsewhere. So I made sure I didn't expand too fast. I just covered my region. We all need sustenance. We all need to be satisfied.

You know those Chinese, they'll eat anything. In famine time they'd eat the brood, the grubs and royal jelly. All protein. Delicious?!

AGING

SMELL: Hinoki.

LLOYD: Bees, they know when to stop having it. They know when to stop.

He moves away from the fräulein.

They do their bit, their work and when it's time, they leave the hive, they fly away and die in the field.

The forager or worker bees they work till all their baby fuzz falls out, their wings get tatty. Their body gets all greasy. I'm greasy.

In the winter the hive shuts down, the workers stop the queen from laying quite so many eggs. She gets tired.

Jean got tired. Scoliosis, arthritis, like the varroa mite, it comes… eventually, over the seas, it comes. It weakens the bee in the late autumn, thus leaving the older bee more prone to infection. The bees are defenceless.

Transition moment.

GRANDSON: Nothing can be done.

The GRANDSON *looks at Jean's things in the boxes. He pulls a notepad out of Lloyd's shirt pocket and flips through the pages. He collects a tray containing a day-of-the-week medication organiser and some bottles of pills and a packet of Depend (adult incontinence pads). He crosses over to Lloyd's armchair.*

He counts the pills into the medication organiser.

Two Panadol, twice a day. Two in the morning, two at night, with meals, A.M. P.M., A.M. P.M., A.M. P.M., A.M. P.M., A.M. P.M., A.M. P.M., A.M. P.M..

One Tritace for blood pressure in the A.M., one, one, one, one, one, one, one.

One Lasix a day for blood pressure and fluid control. Take first thing in the morning, has a diuretic effect. Prepare accordingly. One, two, three, four, five, six, seven.

One asprin in the morning.

One Caltrate a day in the evening before bed (don't mix with dairy products).

Two glucosamine in the morning for joints each A.M.

He spills them as he tries to do this quickly. He realises he's missed one.

One anti-depressant. Zoloft. Morning… Fuck!

DEPEND

The GRANDSON *picks up the packet of Depend nappies and studies it. He pulls a nappy out of the packet.*

GRANDSON: [*reading the packet*] Discreet, underwear likeness, odour control. Five drops out of eight, large. Seven drops out of eight, super large. Nine drops out of eight, super night-time maxi. Quality and comfort assured.

He takes Lloyd's pants off and puts the nappy on. He walks around in it to see what it feels like. He picks up the packet again.

Can hold up to one litre of fluid.

He thinks for a moment and notices a vase of flowers on a table nearby. He pulls out the flowers, puts them to one side and slowly pours the water into the nappy. Once satisfied, he feels inside the nappy and then presses his hand to the floor leaving a wet mark. Revolted, he rips the nappy off and holds it out in front of him.

SMELL: Hinoki fades out.

Through the next section the GRANDSON *takes the remainder of Lloyd's clothes off and dresses in his own clothes. It's a tussle for control.*

I don't want to wear Depend.

LLOYD: Such is life.

GRANDSON: Everything is decaying.

LLOYD: Yeah you've got to focus on the positive.

GRANDSON: You lose your dignity.

LLOYD: We've had our day.

GRANDSON: People think you're 'cute'.

LLOYD: It's quite nice.

GRANDSON: Everything's falling out.

LLOYD: I've got nothing to complain about.

GRANDSON: No animal sits in its own shit.

LLOYD: We all lose our sting.

GRANDSON: Aging is shit. People think you can't make your own decisions.

LLOYD: You can learn lots from us yester-yearers.

GRANDSON: I'm losing you. Time's running out.

LLOYD: It just happens. Pull up your socks! You've got to have a thick skin.

Pause.

PASSING DOWN

The GRANDSON *sits on the ground.*

GRANDSON: How thick is your skin?

Pause.

How did you feel when Dad died?

Silence.

Do you think about him?

Silence.

Tell me what he was like growing up?

Silence.

LLOYD: Oh, well, he… There are many ways to extract but you've got to have the gear to do it.

GRANDSON: How did it feel to sell your bees? Your hundred and fifty hives?

LLOYD: You buy foundation wax and put it in the hive and that would be your starter and then the bees draw the frames out, hundreds of tiny hexagons. They put nectar in the cells. Make life. Then you'd cut the tops off the cells with a hot knife heated by a steam boiler, an old pressure cooker. Then you'd put the frames in the handheld spinner to spin the honey out.

GRANDSON: Grandma's gone.

LLOYD: But the trouble is that meant that you wasted all the efforts of the bees because they had to build the wax again before they could start gathering nectar to turn into honey. In the old days, you'd smoke the bees away, take the comb and honey out and put it into a mosquito net or a cheesecloth and hang it up in the hot sun over time and let it drain into the basin. Lived life.

GRANDSON: No queen, no bees, no honey.

LLOYD: Jean's not up on the hill anymore…

You know, even without the beekeeper, the bees are always out there in the bush, they're always gathering nectar. Such is life.

Here, have this it belonged to your father.

He moves around the granny flat collecting the beekeeping suit, hat, shoes and smoker.

Here, have this, they're just things…

GRANDSON: [*uncertain*] Grandad.

LLOYD: We've had our day. We blow with the wind now.

The GRANDSON *stands with the pile of objects in his arms.*

The GRANDSON *places the hat, smoker and shoes on the ground. He forms the shape of a figure with the objects. The hat where the head should be, the smoker near the hands, the shoes at the feet.*

GRANDSON: What was it like to bury your son?

Silence.

Grandad?

Silence.

Grandad?

LLOYD: You spin the extractor and the central fugal force flings the honey against the sides of the tank, it bleeds down the sides and out the base, the foundation of the tank.

You know, beekeeping evolves from the fact of father and son and/or somebody who'd have a bit of a go. You learn on the way. You're either destined to or…

GRANDSON: Did you expect to give Dad your bees? Or me?

Pause.

LLOYD: Did you want them? [*Beat.*] No, I didn't expect. It's uncertain work; you do a heck of a lot of hard, hot work to get honey.

The GRANDSON *billows the beekeeping suit out onto the ground. It lands between the hat, smoker and shoes as the air slowly drains out.*

GRANDSON: I'll just take some honey this time.

The GRANDSON *collects a jar of honey that is resting nearby on a coffee table. Behind it he notices a random cassette tape, completely out of place. He takes it over to where Lloyd's portable cassette player is beside the armchair. He places the cassette in the recorder, presses play and listens.*

LLOYD: [*voice on the tape player*] This is Lloyd Beckmann Stitz, on the second of the first, two thousand and three. Since my last recording it has been found that my father Wilhelm Stitz had a photograph taken on board a German navel ship called *S.E.Y.D.L.I.T.Z Bremen B.R.E.M.E.N.* at Sydney in August, nineteen hundred and nine. This is the only record I have of my father's entry into Australia, possibly at the port of Brisbane, Queensland. Thank you.

The GRANDSON *stops the tape.*

LIGHTING: The lights fade until only candlelight remains.

The GRANDSON *blows the candle out.*

LIGHTING: Blackout.

THE END

presents

Lloyd Beckmann, Beekeeper

Wednesday 27 April – Sunday 15 May 2011

Devisor/Performer
Tim Stitz

Devisor/Director
Kelly Somes

Lighting Design
Bronwyn Pringle

Composition/Sound Design
Liz Stringer

Sound Design/Realisation
Neddwellyn Jones

Aroma Design
Jodie Ahrens

Design Concept & Realisation
Tim Stitz, Kelly Somes & Ashlee Hughes

Production/Stage Management
Julie Wright

Publicist
Two Blue Cherries/Soulart
Eleanor Howlett

Producer
Two Blue Cherries
Petra Kalive

Dramaturg
Jane Woollard

Photography
Deryk McAlpin, Talya Chalef & Bronwyn Pringle

Artistic Director
Liz Jones

Company Manager
Pippa Bainbridge

Publicist/Education officer
Maureen Hartley

Marketing Coordinator
Louise Jones

Communications Coordinator
Nedd Jones

House Managers
Lisa Höbartner & Rebecca Etchell

Community Outreach
Mary Helen Sassman & Caitlin Dullard

COMMITTEE OF MANAGEMENT:

Catherine Hill, Liz Jones, Duré Dara, Mark Rubbo, Tim Stitz, Caroline Lee, Rhonda Day and Emily Harms.

FRONT OF HOUSE STAFF:

The regular staff and: Liz McColl, Jo-Anne Armstrong, Alicia Benn-Lawler, Mari Lourey, Laurence Strangio, Phil Roberts, Nicola Gunn, Merrilee Moss, Ray Triggs, Tanya Harrowell, Sophie Walsh-Harrington and Annabel Warmington.

La Mama's Committee of Management, Staff and its wider theatrical community acknowledge that our theatre is on traditional Wurundjeri land.

La Mama is financially assisted by the Australian Government through the Australia Council – its Arts Funding and Advisory body - and the Victorian Government through Arts Victoria – Department of Premier and Cabinet, and the Community Support Fund. La Mama productions are financially supported by the City of Melbourne. Our thanks to the Management and staff of Readings Bookshop, Carlton, for their contribution to the running of the Box Office.

Photo by Talya Chalef.

WHY LLOYD?

Lloyd Beckmann Stitz, my paternal grandfather, has played many roles in his life. Committed and doting husband, father and grandfather, hardy worker, survivor of the Depression, learned consumer and aggressive conversationalist. Yet to me he's always been Grandad, the Beekeeper, the ever smiling old Queensland man of the land. Throughout his life he's meticulously and lovingly tended his buzzing colonies and obsessed over the quality of his honey, his own liquid gold. He accepts life for all that it is, complete with its hardships, its joys and pleasures. 'Such is life.'

At times I have found it difficult to fathom his unflappable stiff upper lip. In this piece we've attempted to reconcile Lloyd's ability to bounce back and his refusal to let adversity affect his chipper demeanour. Where are his scars? Tracing four generations of Stitz men and the loss of generational threads within the family was the starting point. Where do we go when the answers about our past cannot be found? What is passed down? What is inherited? What happens when our indefatigable family stalwarts begin to slip further and further towards the inevitable, or tragically depart too soon? And how to combine this story with the mysterious buzzing world of bees to create a piece of theatre?

I wish to pay special tribute to Kelly Somes' unflagging support in developing this work. She is a firm friend, inspired colleague and creative pocket-rocket. To her and everyone who has helped to bring *Beekeeper* to life, including the audiences that saw its early showings, I pay my most humble thanks.

Tim Stitz

Photos by Deryk McAlpin.

TIM STITZ
DEVISOR/PERFORMER

Tim studied at the University of Melbourne and is a graduate of Circle in the Square Theatre School in New York. Recent theatre credits include his sell-out solo-show *Lloyd Beckmann, Beekeeper* (La Mama / Canberra Theatre Centre); *In Other Words* (cheLA, Buenos Aires / Meat Market / Abbotsford Convent); *A Man For All Seasons* (Complete Works); *Prophet & Loss* (Here Theatre); *Three Dog Night* (Two Blue Cherries – Adelaide Festival Centre/ fortyfivedownstairs) and *Asylum* (Here Theatre – La Mama & RAV Tour). At the 2006 Green Room Awards Tim was nominated for Best Male Performer for *Still a Hero* (La Mama) and won the Best Ensemble Award for *The Time Is Not Yet Ripe* (Here Theatre). Tim is a member of Melbourne Playback Theatre Company. Screen credits include *Whatever Happened To That Guy* (Foxtel); *Bogan Pride* (SBS) and the feature film *Dying Breed*. Tim is also chair of the Green Room Awards Independent Theatre Panel and a member of the La Mama Committee of Management.

KELLY SOMES
DEVISOR/DIRECTOR

In 2004, Kelly graduated from the Victorian College of the Arts, School of Drama with a Graduate Diploma in Dramatic Art (Directing). In 2010, Kelly directed a new work by Alison Mann, *She's Not Performing* at La Mama and completed two sell-out seasons of *Lloyd Beckmann, Beekeeper* in Melbourne *(La Mama)* and Canberra *(Canberra Theatre Centre)*. Kelly and collaborators, Tim Stitz and Ashlee Hughes have been nominated for a Green Room Award for Design in the Independent Theatre category. Other recent directing credits include *All My Sleep and Waking* by Mary Rachel Brown, *The Grief Project* for La Mama's 40th Birthday Explorations Season; *Argy Barge* and *Flibberty Gibbet* for St Martins Youth Arts Centre and *The Human Layer*, which was awarded the 2005 Melbourne Fringe Festival Visionary Award.

BRONWYN PRINGLE
LIGHTING DESIGNER

Bronwyn is a freelance lighting designer and technician who has worked around Australia with companies such as Malthouse Theatre, Ballarat Arts Academy, La Mama, Theatre in Decay, Arts Projects Australia, Stuck Pigs Squealing, Here Theatre, Polyglot and more. Projects she has worked on range from large festivals to small developmental pieces in venues that include The Sydney Opera House, a London west end nightclub, the Kuala Lumpur Performing Arts Centre, a warehouse in Buenos Aires, the Federation Square air-conditioning ducts and a woolshed in Glencoe, plus many more conventional and non-conventional theatre spaces. Bronwyn's teaching credits include VCA, NMIT, VUT, The Women's Circus and Monash University. Design highlights include *Triple Bill of Wild Delights* (Finucane & Smith), *Lloyd Beckmann, Beekeeper* (Two Blue Cherries/Soulart Productions), *The Hatpin* (BAA), *In Other Words, Cabaret (*BAA*), The Time Is Not Yet Ripe* (Here Theatre), *Source/Sauce, Catalpa, Site, All My Sleep and Waking* (La Mama), *Asylum* (Here Theatre/La Mama), *Outpatients* (La Mama), Topsy (Here Theatre), *Art for Puppets' Sake* (VCA), *Another Kind of Listening* (La Mama), *4x Beckett* (Stuck Pigs Squealing), *Batboy, Horse Girl Vs Captain Brap* (La Mama), *All of Which are American Dreams* (Theatre in Decay), *Filch* (La Mama) and *Angry Eddie.* Bronwyn has won Green Room Awards for *Letters from Animals* (Here Theatre/SRWT 2007) and *Alias Grace* (Malthouse Theatre 2005), and Fringe Festival design awards for *Anachronisticity* (co-design with Richard Vabre) and *Uninvited Guests* (Design Collaboration Award with Clare

Above and right: photos by Deryk McAlpin.

LIZ STRINGER
COMPOSER/SOUND DESIGNER

Liz is a Melbourne-based songwriter and musician. In 2006, Liz released her debut album *Soon*, followed by the critically acclaimed *Pendulum* (2008) and 2010's *Tides of Time*. Liz has toured extensively throughout Australia, has played major festivals and is a highly sought after session musician. *Lloyd Beckmann, Beekeeper* marks Liz's debut as a composer for the theatre. www.lizstringer.com.

NEDDWELLYN JONES
SOUND DESIGNER/ REALISATION

Throughout the last 5 years, Nedd Jones has composed, created and designed sound for theatre, short film and television. His work has appeared at La Mama under the direction of Laurence Strangio, Nicola Gunn, Emma Valente, Chris Molyneaux, Xanthe Beesley and Lloyd Jones; in television series' *City Homicide* (Seven Network, AU) and *16 and Pregnant* (MTV, US); and in short films by Jono Katz, Dylan Kearney and Nicole Cleary.

JODIE AHRENS
AROMA DESIGNER

Jodie has been driving the multi-sensory work of Roundangle for the past six years. *Tasting Treasure,* an interactive sensory journey for preschoolers is launching at the Melbourne Museum for the 2011 Melbourne Food and Wine Festival. *In the Dark* previewed at the Art of Difference Festival in March 2009. *Deceased Estate* presented at the 2008 Melbourne Fringe Festival won the Melbourne International Arts Festival Award. *Source/Sauce,* an interactive sensory installation developed in collaboration with deaf and deafblind people, won The Visionary Award, The Go Full Tilt Award, The Melbourne International Arts Festival Award (to Sound Artists – Madeleine Flynn and Tim Humphrey) at the 2006 Melbourne Fringe Festival. With her partner, Will, she also runs Our Planet Enterprises – creating and touring environmentally themed performances & workshops.

ASHLEE HUGHES
DESIGN REALISATION

Ashlee is a graduate of the VCA Bachelor of Production. She is currently touring the east coast of Australia as an assistant stage manager on *Cafe Rebetika*. She recently returned from London where she undertook work experience on a film *Miss Mia Miows* in the art department. Last year Ashlee designed *As You Like It* (Winterfall Productions) and *Passage of time within a confined space*. Other recent projects include *Anatomy* (ABC Television), *Don't Be Afraid Of The Dark* (feature film).

JULIE WRIGHT
PRODUCTION/ STAGE MANAGEMENT

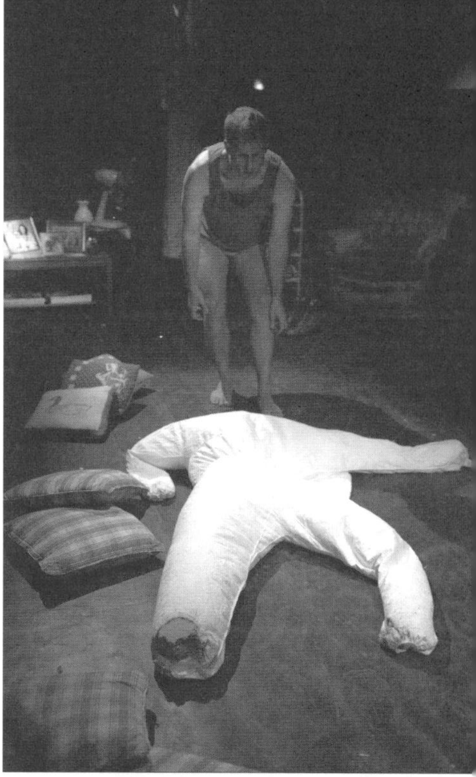

Julie is a graduate of the Victorian College of the Arts (Theatre Production 2004). She has Stage Managed many productions over the years for festivals, theatre, puppetry and dance. Recent productions include; *King John* (The Eleventh Hour & Adelaide International Arts Festival), *Not What I am – Othello Retold* (The Eleventh Hour Theatre), *All My Sleep and Waking* (Soulart Productions), *The Zombie State* (Melbourne Workers Theatre), *Endgame* (The Eleventh Hour & Melbourne International Arts Festival), *Festival Melbourne* (Commonwealth Games Cultural Program).

Photos by Deryk McAlpin.

STANDING OVATION FOR
STATE'S SMALLEST THEATRE

In 2011, La Mama will celebrate 44 years of nurturing new Australian Theatre.

Built in 1883 for Anthony Reuben Ford, a Carlton printer, the building in Faraday Street had been used as a workshop, a boot and shoe factory, an electrical engineering workshop and a silk underwear factory before becoming a theatre in 1967. It was established by Betty Burstall and modelled on experimental theatre activities in New York. Jack Hibberd's play Three Old Friends was the first play performed in the tiny space. Since that time the crowded intimacy of La Mama has provided welcome opportunities to a host of playwrights, actors, directors, technicians, film-makers, poets and comedians, such as David Williamson, Barry Dickins, John Romeril, Tes Lyssiotis, Lloyd Jones, the Cantrills, Judith Lucy, Richard Frankland, Julia Zemiro, and Cate Blanchett... the list of those who have been nurtured there is long.

In 1975 Barry Oakley described La Mama as 'a village phenomenon, a Carlton phenomenon'. Under the capable care of Liz Jones (Artistic Director since 1976), and her La Mama team, approximately 50 productions are produced annually (at La Mama, and the Carlton Courthouse in Drummond Street) and an ever-increasing audience is drawn not only from the Carlton and Melbourne University environs, but from far and wide across the country.

'I set La Mama up, as a space for writers and directors to perform in but also it was a space where people came, as audience, to participate in the creative experiment.'

—Betty Burstall, 1987, Artistic Director of La Mama 1967-76

'Much will be said of La Mama's role in developing a new generation of Australian writing. However, in considering policies and personalities, one should not forget the nature of the space and its impact in making possible performances that would be lost in a large theatre. It gave performances the intimacy of the cinema close-up with the exciting immediacy of the live theatre and the warmth of the coffee lounge.'

—Daryl Wilkinson, 1986, Director
From *La Mama... The story of a Theatre*

La Mama Theatre – which, on various occasions, has been called headquarters, the source, the shopfront and the birthplace of Australian theatre – was classified by the National Trust in 1999.

'The two story brick building is of State cultural significance because it has been occupied by La Mama Theatre... The building is indelibly associated with the performance arts and is a rare manifestation of an experimental theatre in Australia...'

—National Trust Classification Report

When it comes to grassroots Melbourne theatre, La Mama in Carlton is like the 60GB iPod – small, subtle, but containing a whole lot more than you might expect.

—John Bailey, The *Age*. E.G. 29/06/05

La Mama produces work from two venues: 205 Faraday Street, Carlton (opposite top), and at the La Mama Courthouse, 349 Drummond Street, Carlton.

Photos by Talya Chalef.